FOOTBALL WORLD
LEAGUES

James Nixon

FRANKLIN WATTS
LONDON • SYDNEY

Franklin Watts
First published in Great Britain in 2017 by The Watts Publishing Group

Credits
Editor: James Nixon
Design: Keith Williams, sprout.uk.com
Planning and production by Discovery Books Limited

Photo credits: Cover image: Getty Images (Mark Leech Sports Photography).
Getty Images: pp. 4 (John Peters), 5 top (Visual China Group), 5 bottom (Michael Dodge), 6 (IAN KINGTON/AFP), 8 (IAN KINGTON/AFP), 9 (Nathan Stirk), 11 (Alex Livesey), 12 (Mark Runnacles), 13 (Ian MacNicol), 16 (Boris Streubel), 20 top (Dave Winter/Icon Sport), 21 bottom (FRANCK FIFE/AFP), 23 top (Valery Matytsin\TASS), 27 (George Frey), 29 bottom-right (Popperfoto).
Shutterstock: pp. 7 top (almonfoto), 7 bottom (Mitch Gunn), 7 bottom (daykung), 14 top (Marcos Mesa Sam Wordley), 15 top (Christian Bertrand), 15 bottom (Maxisport), 17 top (Ververidis Vasilis), 17 bottom (AGIF), 18 (Fabrizio Andrea Bertani), 19 top (Marco Iacobucci EPP), 19 bottom (Paolo Bona), 21 top (Vlad1988), 22 top (mr3002), 22 bottom (Bruno Monico), 23 bottom (CP DC Press), 25 bottom (lev radin), 28 (A.RICARDO), 29 bottom-left (Jefferson Bernardes).
Wikimedia: pp. 10 (joshjdss), 20 bottom, 24 (Yohames), 25 top (ArtBrom), 26 (Erica McCaulley), 29 top (ianjvoos).

ISBN 978 1 4451 5580 7

Printed in China

FIFE COUNCIL	
155990	
PETERS	12-Dec-2017
J796.334	£12.99
JSPO	BANA

Franklin Watts
An imprint of
Hachette Children's Group
Part of The Watts Publishing Group
Carmelite House
50 Victoria Embankment
London EC4Y 0DZ

An Hachette UK Company
www.hachette.co.uk

www.franklinwatts.co.uk

The statistics in this book were correct at the time of printing, but because of the nature of sport, it cannot be guaranteed that they are now accurate.

Every effort has been made by the Publishers to ensure that the websites in this book are suitable for children, that they are of the highest educational value, and that they contain no inappropriate or offensive material. However, because of the nature of the Internet, it is impossible to guarantee that the contents of these sites will not be altered. We strongly advise that Internet access is supervised by a responsible adult.

CONTENTS

THE GLOBAL GAME

Nicknamed 'the beautiful game', football has become the most popular sport on the globe. There are now leagues in over 200 countries, in which clubs challenge to be their nation's best.

How it works

Clubs from each country are grouped together into league **divisions**. The national league champion is the winner of the highest division. In each division, the winner is the team that scores the most points and finishes highest in the table. Points are awarded for wins and draws. Teams can be **promoted** or **relegated** to a higher or lower division.

Over the course of a season, teams usually play every other team in their league twice (home and away), in what is called a double **round robin**.

Transfer system

The English league doesn't just contain English players; it contains a mixture of footballers from across the world. This is because players can be **transferred** between clubs in different countries. The best footballers on the planet come at a high price. To sign these players, teams usually have to offer high wages and pay the selling club an expensive fee.

Manchester United signed French star Paul Pogba (right) from Italian side Juventus for a world record fee of £89 million in 2016.

THE BIG FIVE

The English Premier League, La Liga in Spain, the Bundesliga in Germany, Serie A in Italy and Ligue 1 in France are rated as the top five European leagues and the best in the world. These leagues contain the wealthiest, most successful clubs and the world's top players.

The developing game

Europe may have the big leagues but the game continues to grow around the world. For example, the Chinese Super League was created in 2004 and expanded to a 16-team league in 2008. China is a rich country, and its clubs have recently been able to attract star players and managers. However, teams are not allowed to field more than five foreign players. This gives Chinese footballers a chance to play and develop.

The A-League was also founded in 2004. It contains nine teams from Australia and one from New Zealand. The A-League's format is unusual – the top six sides qualify for a **knockout** competition in which the champions are eventually decided in a head-to-head Grand Final.

Brazilian World Cup-winning coach Luiz Felipe Scolari (centre) led Guangzhou Evergrande to Chinese Super League titles in 2015 and 2016.

Melbourne Victory score a goal past Western Sydney Wanderers in the A-League.

5

THE PREMIER LEAGUE

Known for its speed and excitement, the English Premier League is the most-watched football league on the planet. The matches are broadcast in over 200 countries to a potential audience of 4.7 billion people. The Premier League is also the richest league in the world.

The rules

The top division of English football was renamed the Premier League in 1992. Like many leagues, the 20 clubs play each other twice, with 3 points awarded for a win and one point for a draw. If two or more teams are level on points they are ranked by **goal difference**, then goals scored.

At the end of the season, the top four teams qualify for next season's **UEFA Champions League** competition. The fifth-placed team qualifies for the **UEFA Europa League**. Finishing in the bottom-three spells disaster: these clubs are relegated down to the next division.

Leicester City do battle with 2016 Premier League runners up Tottenham.

The challengers

Out of the 47 teams that have taken part since the Premier League was formed, there have only been six winners – Manchester United, Blackburn Rovers, Arsenal, Chelsea, Manchester City and Leicester City. In the 2000s, the top four positions were dominated by the 'big four' – Arsenal, Chelsea, Liverpool and Manchester United. But since then, Manchester City and Tottenham Hotspur have become strong challengers. Then from nowhere, Leicester shocked the football world to win the title in 2016.

Record makers

Alan Shearer holds the record for the most goals ever scored in the Premier League. The striker scored 260 goals in 441 Premier League appearances and helped Blackburn win the league in 1995. The former Manchester United winger Ryan Giggs (left) holds the record for the most Premier League appearances. During his 632 games, he scored in the first 21 seasons of the league.

CLUB FOCUS

Manchester United, nicknamed the Red Devils, are one of the most widely supported football teams in the world. They have easily been the most successful Premier League club in history. They won the very first Premier League in 1993 and won their 13th title in 2013. Every title was won with legendary manager Sir Alex Ferguson (right) in charge. The 2013 victory was Ferguson's final season. Manchester United's home, Old Trafford, is the largest club stadium in English football with a capacity of 75,643.

ROLL OF HONOUR

2007	2008	2009	2010	2011	2012	2013	2014	2015	2016	2017
Manchester United	Manchester United	Manchester United	Chelsea	Manchester United	Manchester City	Manchester United	Manchester City	Chelsea	Leicester City	Chelsea

The Premier League trophy has a golden crown at the top.

THE CHAMPIONSHIP

The second division of English football has been called The Championship since 2004. This is where 24 clubs battle to reach the Premier League every season. The Championship has the highest **attendance** figures for a second division in the world.

Moving on up

At the end of the season, the top two teams in the league are automatically promoted to the Premier League. The clubs that finish from third down to sixth enter a **play-off** competition. The play-offs decide which club will grab that final promotion spot. In the play-off semi-finals, the third-placed team play the sixth-placed team and the fourth-placed team face the fifth-placed team. The semi-finals are played over two **legs**, in which the clubs play home and away, and the winners are decided on an **aggregate** score.

Hull City score the winning goal in their 1-0 play-off final victory against Sheffield Wednesday in 2016.

The play-off final

Gaining that last promotion place all comes down to one match in a nerve-racking showdown at Wembley Stadium, London. Due to the great riches on offer in the Premier League, winning the play-off final is often said to have the biggest prize in football. If the scores are still level after **extra time** the winner is decided by a **penalty shoot-out**.

Norwich City's young star Jacob Murphy (left) looks to fire the club back to the Premier League again.

TALES FROM HISTORY

Finishing third in the league after a long, hard season and missing out on promotion is tough. In 1993, Portsmouth missed out on automatic promotion because they scored just one less goal over the whole season than second-placed West Ham. Portsmouth then lost in the play-offs and had to wait another ten years to get promoted. In 1994, it was Millwall that finished third but lost in the play-offs. Over 20 years later, Millwall have still yet to reach the Premier League!

Yo-yo clubs

The gap in quality and wealth between the Premier League and the Championship makes life hard for promoted sides. Teams that are constantly getting promoted but relegated back down again are called yo-yo clubs. Birmingham City have been promoted or relegated between the top two divisions a record 24 times! Norwich City are a modern yo-yo club – they hold the record with Crystal Palace as the most relegated team from the Premier League (4 times).

ROLL OF HONOUR

2005	2006	2007	2008	2009	2010	2011	2012	2013	2014	2015	2016	2017
Sunderland	Reading	Sunderland	West Bromwich Albion	Wolverhampton Wanderers	Newcastle United	QPR	Reading	Cardiff City	Leicester City	Bournemouth	Burnley	Newcastle United

FA WOMEN'S SUPER LEAGUE

Founded in 2010, the Women's Super League (WSL) is the top women's football league in England. The league, which replaced the Women's Premier League, is made up of two divisions – WSL 1 and WSL 2 – with ten teams competing in each.

An expanding league

When the WSL began there were just eight teams in one division. Since 2014 the league has expanded quickly. In that year WSL 2 was added as a ten-team league with promotion up for grabs to WSL 1. Sheffield FC were added to the WSL league system in 2016. They qualified by beating Portsmouth 1-0 in a dramatic play-off final. In 2017, Brighton & Hove Albion are set to join the league. The plan is to eventually have 24 clubs in the WSL.

CLUB FOCUS

Arsenal Ladies are by far the most successful club in the history of English women's football. They were formed in 1987. Since the foundation of the Women's Premier League in 1992 Arsenal have won 14 English league titles including two WSL titles. Incredibly, between 2004 and 2012 they won nine titles in a row. Arsenal are also the only British side to ever win the UEFA Women's Champions League, beating Swedish club Umeå IK in the final in 2007.

Veteran winger Rachel Yankey (left) has been winning titles with Arsenal since 2006.

Quick success

Manchester City were one of the teams who entered the WSL during the 2014 expansion. In just three seasons they became the English league champions. Helped by the signings of England captain Steph Houghton and England goalkeeper Karen Bardsley, Manchester City went the whole 2016 WSL season unbeaten and only conceded four goals! They clinched the title by beating second-placed and defending champions Chelsea 2-0. City's Scottish striker Jane Ross ended the season as the division's top scorer.

Record scorers

In the opening season of WSL 1, Rachel Williams scored 14 times in 14 appearances for Birmingham City as they were pipped to the title by Arsenal. Nobody has scored more goals in a WSL 1 season since. Natasha Dowie came close, scoring 13 in 14 games to help Liverpool win the league in 2013.

Jane Ross in Women's Super League action against Birmingham City.

ROLL OF HONOUR

Arsenal	2011
Arsenal	2012
Liverpool	2013
Liverpool	2014
Chelsea	2015
Manchester City	2016

SCOTTISH PREMIERSHIP

All the countries that make up the UK have their own leagues. The top league in Scotland has a strong history. It was renamed the Scottish Premiership in 2013.

St Johnstone forward Graham Cummins wins an aerial duel in a match against Hearts.

Split season

Since 2001, the Scottish top division has contained 12 clubs. Every season is divided into two phases. After each club has played each other three times, the league is split into two – the 'top six' and the 'bottom six'. Each team then plays the other five clubs in their section once. This means every team plays 38 games, the same as many other European leagues including the Premier League.

Relegation play-off

In Scotland, only the champions qualify for next season's UEFA Champions League. Second and third enter the Europa League. The bottom-placed team is automatically relegated to the Scottish Championship (second divsion). The club that finishes 11th faces a relegation play-off over two legs against a highly placed team from the Scottish Championship. It is a game of survival – win and they stay up, lose and they go down.

ROLL OF HONOUR

2007	2008	2009	2010	2011	2012	2013	2014	2015	2016	2017
Celtic	Celtic	Rangers	Rangers	Rangers	Celtic	Celtic	Celtic	Celtic	Celtic	Celtic

The giants of Glasgow

Celtic and Rangers, both from the city of Glasgow, have dominated Scottish football. In the history of the top divison, Rangers have won 54 titles and Celtic 48! In the remaining 19 seasons, nine other clubs have been champions. The last time a club other than Rangers or Celtic won the title was when Sir Alex Ferguson guided Aberdeen to victory in 1985!

Together, Celtic and Rangers are known as the 'Old Firm'. They make up one of the fiercest rivalries in world football.

CLUB FOCUS

Celtic are the top club in Scotland today, winning the last six league championships. They still have some way to go to beat the nine titles they won in a row between 1966 and 1974. This was Celtic's greatest period under the management of Jock Stein. In 1967 they also became the first British club to win the **European Cup**, the trophy now awarded to the Champions League winners. Celtic are estimated to have around nine million fans worldwide and their stadium, Celtic Park, is the largest in Scotland.

Rangers (blue) and Celtic (green) have played each other over 400 times!

LA LIGA

The Spanish top division is called La Liga and is often rated as the world's best league. La Liga's 20 clubs attract many of the game's star players and showcase an astonishing amount of skill and flair.

Top dog

According to UEFA, La Liga has been the top league in Europe for the past five years. La Liga clubs have won more Champions Leagues (16) and more Europa Leagues (10) than those from any other league. It has also produced the most **Ballon d'Or** winners (19), given to Europe's best player each year.

Goal machines

Lionel Messi, Barcelona's Argentine maestro, has the all-time goalscoring record in La Liga. In his 382 appearances, Messi has found the net an incredible 349 times, and still counting. Not far behind is Real Madrid's Portuguese goal machine Cristiano Ronaldo. He has scored 285 times in just 265 La Liga games.

Stat Tracker

	Titles	Runners up
Real Madrid	33	23
Barcelona	24	25
Atlético Madrid	10	8
Athletic Bilbao	8	7
Valencia	6	6
Real Sociedad	2	3
Deportivo La Coruña	1	5
Sevilla	1	4
Real Betis	1	0

Four-time Ballon d'Or winner Cristiano Ronaldo in action against Atlético Madrid.

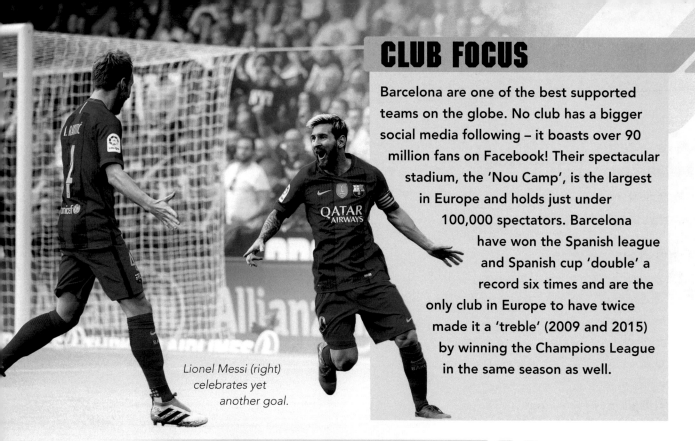

CLUB FOCUS

Barcelona are one of the best supported teams on the globe. No club has a bigger social media following – it boasts over 90 million fans on Facebook! Their spectacular stadium, the 'Nou Camp', is the largest in Europe and holds just under 100,000 spectators. Barcelona have won the Spanish league and Spanish cup 'double' a record six times and are the only club in Europe to have twice made it a 'treble' (2009 and 2015) by winning the Champions League in the same season as well.

Lionel Messi (right) celebrates yet another goal.

ROLL OF HONOUR

2007	2008	2009	2010	2011	2012	2013	2014	2015	2016	2017
Real Madrid	Real Madrid	Barcelona	Barcelona	Barcelona	Real Madrid	Barcelona	Atlético Madrid	Barcelona	Barcelona	Real Madrid

TALES FROM HISTORY

Barcelona and Real Madrid have both assembled some pretty amazing squads in their histories. Dutch legend Johan Cruyff managed Barcelona to four La Liga titles in a row between 1991 and 1994. His side, starring Dutch defender Ronald Koeman and Danish playmaker Michael Laudrup, was known as the *Dream Team*.

In the early 2000s, Real Madrid snapped up as many global superstars as they could. David Beckham (right), Luis Figo the Portuguese wonder winger, Brazil's star striker Ronaldo and French midfielder Zinedine Zidane all arrived for big fees. The players were nicknamed the Galacticos and helped Real Madrid win the 2003 league title.

BUNDESLIGA

The Bundesliga is the top division of German football. It is currently ranked as the second-best league in Europe and is the highest-attended football league on the planet. The average attendance of a Bundesliga match is a whopping 43,300!

Star-rated teams

The Bundesliga was founded in 1963 and is contested by 18 clubs. Hamburg is the only team to have played in every season of the Bundesliga, yet they have only won three titles. In the last few years, Bayern Munich have risen to dominance winning every title between 2013 and 2016.

To honour their Bundesliga titles, players from certain clubs wear gold stars on their jerseys. If a club has won 20 Bundesligas the players wear four stars. One star is awarded for three titles, two stars for five titles, and three stars for ten titles.

Star Tracker

Club	Titles	Stars
Bayern Munich	27	★★★★
Borussia Mönchengladbach	5	★★
Borussia Dortmund	5	★★
Werder Bremen	4	★
Hamburg	3	★
VFB Stuttgart	3	★

Thomas Müller (right) shoots for Bayern Munich against 2004 champions Werder Bremen.

CLUB FOCUS

Bayern Munich are the most successful and popular German club. As well as 27 Bundesligas, they have won 18 national cups and five European Cup trophies. These included three European Cups in a row between 1974 and 1976, the last time any club achieved this feat. Bayern Munich's Champions League victory in 2013 landed them the league, national cup, and European Cup treble – a first for a German team. In 2014, they went on a record run of 53 Bundesliga matches without defeat! Today they can count on their awesome number-one Manuel Neuer (below), who has been voted the World's Best Goalkeeper.

Fan-tastic

The large crowds set up an incredible atmosphere. At Borussia Dortmund's stadium, named Signal Iduna Park, over 80,000 fans fill the stadium for every match (above). This gives Dortmund the highest average attendance for any football club in the world.

The Bomber

German and Bayern Munich legend Gerd Müller comfortably holds the record for the most Bundesliga goals. Nicknamed 'The Bomber', Müller, a classic **goalpoacher**, scored 365 times in 427 games in the 1960s and 1970s. Müller won the top scorer prize in seven separate seasons, and in 1970, he scored in a record 16 league games in a row!

ROLL OF HONOUR

2007	2008	2009	2010	2011	2012	2013	2014	2015	2016	2017
VFB Stuttgart	Bayern Munich	Wolfsburg	Bayern Munich	Borussia Dortmund	Borussia Dortmund	Bayern Munich	Bayern Munich	Bayern Munich	Bayern Munich	Bayern Munich

SERIE A

Serie A is Italy's top football division and has been in operation since 1929. It contains some of the most technically gifted players in world football. The league is known for its high-quality passing and its tactical and defensive style of games.

The seven sisters

Juventus, AC Milan, Inter Milan, Roma, Lazio, Napoli and Fiorentina are regarded as the top clubs in Serie A. Together they are known as the 'seven sisters'. These clubs are regular challengers for the title. Inter are the only club to have played in every Serie A season since 1929! Roma and Juventus have each been relegated for just one season.

CLUB FOCUS

Juventus, from the city of Turin, are Italy's most successful club and have been champions six times in a row between 2012 and 2017. Overall they have won a record 33 league titles and a record 11 Italian cups. Nicknamed 'The Old Lady', Juventus are in fact the only club in football history to have won every international competition possible. The club is estimated to have a staggering 180 million fans worldwide. In 2014, Juventus won Serie A with a record 102 points and 33 victories. The next two seasons saw Juventus become the first Italian team to complete back-to-back league and cup doubles.

Inter Milan's first kit is striped black and blue while Juventus play in back and white stripes.

Roma's Radja Nainggolan (red) and Lazio's Lucas Biglia (pale blue) fight for the ball in a hotly contested Rome derby.

Derby days

Many of Italy's top clubs have a big rival from the same city. When two clubs from the same city or area play each other, these games are known as **derbies**.

The Rome derby between Lazio and Roma is one of the most intense rivalries in Europe. Their shared ground is at the Stadio Olimpico. AC Milan and Inter Milan have won 18 Serie A titles each and also share a home and a derby at the 80,000-capacity San Siro stadium.

Maldini the great

Paolo Maldini (right) was one of the greatest defenders of all time. He spent all 25 seasons of his career at AC Milan until he retired at the age of 41 in 2009. In that time he played a record 647 games in Serie A.

ROLL OF HONOUR

2007	2008	2009	2010	2011	2012	2013	2014	2015	2016	2017
Inter Milan	Inter Milan	Inter Milan	Inter Milan	AC Milan	Juventus	Juventus	Juventus	Juventus	Juventus	Juventus

LIGUE 1

The highest football division in France is called Ligue 1. It was established in 1932 and is currently ranked as the fifth best league in Europe.

Past champs

A variety of clubs have dominated Ligue 1 at different times. Saint-Étienne hold the record for the most championships. Seven out of their ten victories came in the 1960s and 1970s. Marseille are one behind with nine titles. Their golden era was the late-1980s and early-1990s. In the 2000s, Lyon went on an amazing run, winning seven league titles in a row between 2002 and 2008.

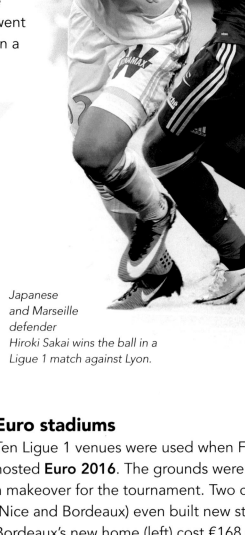

Japanese and Marseille defender Hiroki Sakai wins the ball in a Ligue 1 match against Lyon.

⚽ Stat Tracker

	Titles	Runners up
Saint-Étienne	10	3
Marseille	9	12
Nantes	8	7
Monaco	8	6
Lyon	7	4
Reims	6	3
Bordeaux	6	9
Paris Saint-Germain	6	8
Nice	4	3
Lille	3	6

Euro stadiums

Ten Ligue 1 venues were used when France hosted **Euro 2016**. The grounds were given a makeover for the tournament. Two clubs (Nice and Bordeaux) even built new stadiums. Bordeaux's new home (left) cost €168 million to build and is one of the most unusual but beautiful-looking stadiums in the world.

CLUB FOCUS

Today's dominant force in French football is Paris Saint-Germain (PSG). They have won every Ligue 1 title between 2013 and 2016. The club was only formed in 1970, yet they have triumphed in 31 different competitions since then, making them the most successful team in French history. Their top players include Italian playmaker Marco Verratti, Argentinian winger Ángel Di Mariá (right) and the striker Edinson Cavani from Uruguay. Paris Saint-Germain is the second most popular club in France after Marseille. Matches between these two giants are called *Les Classiques* (The Classics).

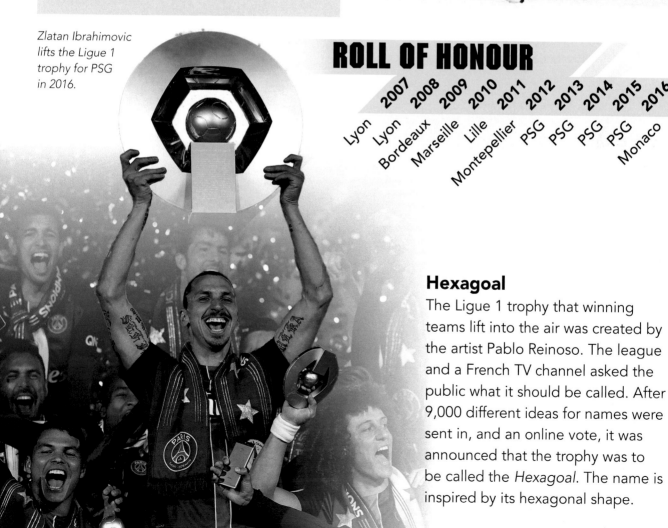

Zlatan Ibrahimovic lifts the Ligue 1 trophy for PSG in 2016.

ROLL OF HONOUR

2007	2008	2009	2010	2011	2012	2013	2014	2015	2016	2017
Lyon	Lyon	Bordeaux	Marseille	Lille	Montepellier	PSG	PSG	PSG	PSG	Monaco

Hexagoal

The Ligue 1 trophy that winning teams lift into the air was created by the artist Pablo Reinoso. The league and a French TV channel asked the public what it should be called. After 9,000 different ideas for names were sent in, and an online vote, it was announced that the trophy was to be called the *Hexagoal*. The name is inspired by its hexagonal shape.

MORE EURO LEAGUES

Outside the big five leagues of Europe, other clubs have produced fine teams and triumphed in international competitions.

Eredivisie

The Dutch top flight called the Eredivsie was formed in 1956 and contains 18 teams. Astonishingly, apart from 1981, 2009 and 2010, every Eredivisie season since 1965 has been won by one of the big three Netherlands clubs. Ajax Amsterdam have won a record 33 titles; 2016 winners PSV Eindhoven have won 18 times, and Feyenoord from Rotterdam are ten-time champions.

The 'big three' Dutch clubs are also all past European Cup winners. Former Ajax forward Johan Cruyff was named European Player of the Century in 1999. He helped Ajax win three European Cups in a row from 1971 to 1973.

ROLL OF HONOUR

2007	2008	2009	2010	2011	2012	2013	2014	2015	2016	2017
PSV Eindhoven	PSV Eindhoven	AZ Alkmaar	Twente	Ajax	Ajax	Ajax	Ajax	PSV Eindhoven	PSV Eindhoven	Feyenoord

Ajax players celebrate a goal.

Primeira Liga

The Portuguese Primeira Liga is another 18-club league dominated by three clubs. A total of 70 teams have competed in the Primeira Liga but only five have ever become champions. In fact Benfica (36 titles), Porto (27) and Sporting Lisbon (18) have won in every season bar Belenenses' victory in 1946 and Boavista's in 2001!

ROLL OF HONOUR

2007	2008	2009	2010	2011	2012	2013	2014	2015	2016	2017
Porto	Porto	Porto	Benfica	Porto	Porto	Porto	Benfica	Benfica	Benfica	Benfica

Portuguese international André Almeida sets off on a dribble for Benfica.

Russian Premier League

The Russian Premier League was formed in 2001 and is quickly becoming one of the strongest leagues in Europe. The division has 16 clubs – the top two finishers qualify for the Champions League while the bottom two are relegated to the division below.

CSKA Moscow (black) pipped Rostov (yellow) to the 2016 Russian Premier League title on the final day of the season.

ROLL OF HONOUR

2006	2007	2008	2009	2011	2012	2013	2014	2015	2016	2017
CSKA Moscow	Zenit Saint Petersburg	Rubin Kazan	Rubin Kazan	Zenit Saint Petersburg	Zenit Saint Petersburg	CSKA Moscow	CSKA Moscow	Zenit Saint Petersburg	CSKA Moscow	Spartak Moscow

Belgian First Division

The Belgian First Division has recently produced a remarkable crop of players. The Belgium national team topped the **FIFA World Rankings** for the first time in November 2015. Eden Hazard, Kevin De Bruyne (right), Romelu Lukaku, Vincent Kompany, and goalkeeper Thibaut Courtouis are just a few of Belgium's stars now playing in the English Premier League.

After the regular season the Belgian First Division has a unique play-off system. The top six sides play each other again twice. The points that clubs win in these games are added to half of their regular season points to find the winner! Anderlecht have won a record 34 titles since the league's formation in 1895.

ROLL OF HONOUR

2007	2008	2009	2010	2011	2012	2013	2014	2015	2016	2017
Anderlecht	Standard Liège	Standard Liège	Anderlecht	Genk	Anderlecht	Anderlecht	Anderlecht	Gent	Club Brugge	Anderlecht

MAJOR LEAGUE SOCCER

Major League Soccer (MLS) is football's highest league across the United States and Canada. Twenty teams fight it out for the league title – 17 from the US and three from Canada. Unlike most top flights, there is no relegation.

Conference system

Because of the huge distances between the MLS clubs, the league is split into an Eastern and Western Conference (below). Each club plays 24 matches against their own conference plus ten matches against teams from the other conference. The top six sides in each conference qualify for the MLS Cup play-offs. The play-offs are where the MLS winner is decided.

Play-off system

In the play-offs, the six qualifiers in each conference battle to be conference champions. The conference semi-finals and finals are two-leg games. If an aggregate score is tied the winner is the team who scored more away goals. If there is still a tie, extra time and penalties are used. The end-of-season climax is a single match play-off final between the Eastern and Western Conference champions.

- Vancouver Whitecaps FC
- Seattle Sounders FC
- Portland Timbers
- Montreal Impact
- New England Revolution
- Toronto FC
- New York City FC
- Real Salt Lake
- Chicago Fire
- New York Red Bulls
- San Jose Earthquakes
- Philadelphia Union
- Columbus Crew SC
- Colorado Rapids
- D.C. United
- Sporting Kansas City
- LA Galaxy
- FC Dallas
- Houston Dynamo
- Orlando City SC

Conference
- Eastern
- Western

Seattle Sounders' spectacular stadium was built in 2002, seven years before they joined MLS. In 2016, the Sounders won their first MLS title.

Expansion

The first MLS season took place in 1996 with ten teams bidding for glory. D.C. United from Washington were victorious and won three out of the first four titles. As the US game has grown more popular the league has steadily expanded. In 2007, Toronto FC were the first Canadian team to join. In 2018, there will be 24 teams. Los Angeles Galaxy have the best record among MLS clubs. They have won the most MLS titles (5) and have made the most appearances in the play-offs (16).

The salary cap

MLS is exciting and unpredictable. Teams are evenly matched due to the salary cap. The salary cap means clubs are only allowed to pay their squad of 20 players a limited amount of money. This prevents teams hoarding all of the best players. The rules now allow clubs to spend extra money on three 'designated players'. This has made it possible for teams to bring some world superstars to MLS. David Beckham was MLS's first designated player to sign up when he joined LA Galaxy in 2007.

New York City entered MLS in 2015 and announced Spanish star David Villa (left) and Englishman Frank Lampard (right) as its first two designated players.

ROLL OF HONOUR

2007	2008	2009	2010	2011	2012	2013	2014	2015	2016
Houston Dynamo	Columbus Crew	Real Salt Lake	Colorado Rapids	LA Galaxy	LA Galaxy	Sporting Kansas City	LA Galaxy	Portland Timbers	Seattle Sounders

NATIONAL WOMEN'S SOCCER LEAGUE

The United States is one of the top countries in the world for women's football. The US women's national team is currently ranked number one in the world. All of the current US squad play their football in the professional National Women's Soccer League (NWSL).

How it works

The NWSL started in 2013 with just eight clubs. Houston Dash and Orlando Pride joined to make it ten teams in the 2016 season. The season runs through the summer from April to September with each side playing ten away games and ten at home. The team that comes top of the table wins the NSWL Shield, but not the NWSL title. The top four sides go on to compete in a play-off to be champions.

The rosters

Each team is allowed 20 players on their **roster** (squad). Like men's football in the US, a salary cap is in place to make the league fair and entertaining. The NWSL goes even further to make the teams equal. Every club is allocated an even number of players from the US, Canadian and Mexican national teams.

Washington Spirit (red) face Western New York Flash in the first ever season of the NWSL.

The draft

In January, before every season, all of the clubs take part in the NWSL College **Draft**. At the draft, teams choose from a list, the junior players that they want to join their squads next season. There are four rounds of player picks. The order the teams choose depends on where they finished the season before. The bottom-placed team gets to choose first! In 2016, Portland Thorns selected the outstanding US defender Emily Sonnett as the number-one pick.

NWSL history

The club that has won the NWSL Shield has never gone on to achieve play-off glory. Seattle Reign won the shield two years running in 2014 and 2015, but in both seasons were beaten in the play-off final by Kansas City. 2016 was Western New York Flash's lucky year. They sneaked in to the play-offs as the fourth qualifiers, and then triumphed over Washington Spirit in the final in a penalty shoot-out.

Emily Sonnett (left) in action for the United States national team.

⚽ Stat Tracker

	Titles	Runners up	Shields	Play-offs
Kansas City	2	0	0	3
Western New York Flash	1	1	1	2
Portland Thorns	1	0	1	3
Seattle Reign	0	2	2	2
Washington Spirit	0	1	0	3
Chicago Red Stars	0	0	0	2
Sky Blue FC	0	0	0	1
Boston Breakers	0	0	0	0
Houston Dash	0	0	0	0
Orlando Pride	0	0	0	0

THE BRASILEIRÃO

Brazil is a football-crazy country with some of the most passionate fans on the globe. Brazil's top national league is called the Brasileirão. It is one of the strongest leagues in the world and has produced many of the game's greatest talents.

A world-class league

Each season, four out of the 20 Brasileirão clubs are relegated. The top four qualify for the **Copa Libertadores**, which is like the Champions League, but for clubs in South America and Mexico. The winners of the Copa Libertadores enter the FIFA Club World Cup, which crowns the club champion of the world. Clubs from the Brasileirão have won the Club World Cup four times.

Corinthians (white) keep the ball from Flamengo (red and black) during their victorious 2015 season.

Past winners

Since the Brasileirão began in 1959, a staggering 156 clubs have contested the league. Seventeen of these teams have become champions. In 2016, Palmeiras became the most successful club by winning their ninth Brasileirão title. Santos have won eight times. Corinthians won their sixth title in 2015, the same number that has been won by São Paulo.

ROLL OF HONOUR

2007	2008	2009	2010	2011	2012	2013	2014	2015	2016
São Paulo	São Paulo	Flamengo	Fluminense	Corinthians	Fluminense	Cruzeiro	Cruzeiro	Corinthians	Palmeiras

The Maracana

The Maracana in Rio de Janeiro is one of the most iconic and famous stadiums in the world and the largest in Brazil. It was built for the 1950 World Cup and hosted the final in front of almost 200,000 fans! Today, Fluminense and Flamengo play their home games at the Maracana. It is now an all-seater stadium with a capacity of 78,639. In 2014, the Maracana hosted the World Cup final for a second time and it was also the venue for the 2016 Olympic opening and closing ceremonies.

Superstars

The Brazilian national league has developed some of football's greatest players, such as 2002 World Cup winners, Ronaldo, Rivaldo and Ronaldinho. European clubs snap up these talents, often at a young age. Barcelona star Neymar (left) was signed as a 21-year-old from Santos for £48.6 million!

TALES FROM HISTORY

Between 1961 and 1965 Santos won five Brazilian championships in a row, a feat that remains unequalled today. The team was nicknamed *The Santastics* and is considered to be one of the strongest club sides in the history of football. They were led by the game's greatest player ever – Pelé. Pelé scored an extraordinary 470 league goals in 412 games for Santos. His 541 goals in top-division football is a world record.

The Santastics *of 1962. Pelé sits on the bottom row, second from right.*

GLOSSARY

aggregate the total score between two teams that have played two legs or more

attendance the number of fans who have watched a game in the stadium

Ballon d'Or a prize awarded every year to the best male player in Europe. Ballon d'Or means Golden Ball in English.

Copa Libertadores an annual competition contested between the top clubs in the leagues of South America and Mexico

derby a match between two rival teams from the same area

division a group of teams joined together for a league competition

draft an annual event where the clubs in a league select junior players to become part of their squads

Euro 2016 the European Championships competition held in 2016, contested by the nations of Europe

European Cup the former name for the tournament now known as the Champions League

extra time thirty added minutes when the score is tied after ninety minutes

FIFA World Rankings a ranking system for men's national football teams based on game results. FIFA is the International Federation of Association Football.

goal difference the difference between the amount of goals a team has scored and the amount they have let in (conceded)

goalpoacher a scorer of lots of close-range goals

knockout a tournament in which the losers at each stage are eliminated

legs the matches played between two clubs that decide which team advances to the next stage of a competition

penalty shoot-out five penalty kicks for each side, each to be taken by a different player

play-offs extra knockout matches to decide the outcome of a competition

promoted moved to a higher division for the following season

relegated moved to a lower division for the next season

roster a list of players at a club available for team selection

round robin a competition in which each team plays every other team in turn

transferred moved from one football club to play for another

UEFA Champions League an annual competition contested by the top clubs from the leagues around Europe. UEFA is the Union of European Football Associations.

UEFA Europa League an annual competition for European clubs that have performed well in their national leagues and cups

FURTHER INFORMATION

BOOKS

An Infographic Guide to: Football,
Wayland, 2016

The Football Encyclopedia,
Clive Gifford, Kingfisher, 2016

Greatest Fans (Planet Football),
Clive Gifford, Wayland, 2017

*Top of the League: Football Facts
and Terrific Trivia*,
Andrea Mills, QED Publishing, 2016

WEBSITES

www.fourfourtwo.com
Includes the latest news and features such as
the 'Greatest Premier League Games Ever'.

www.footballsgreatest.weebly.com/club-teams
Read about 20 of the greatest club teams of
all time.

www.bbc.co.uk/sport/football/tables
Keep track of who is top of the table in
leagues around the world.

www.myfootballfacts.com/world_football_
leagues.html
This site contains a mountain of stats, including
past league champions and top goalscorers.

INDEX

FOOTBALL WORLD

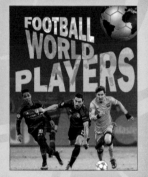
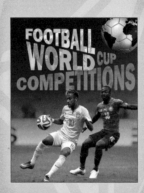
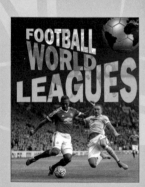